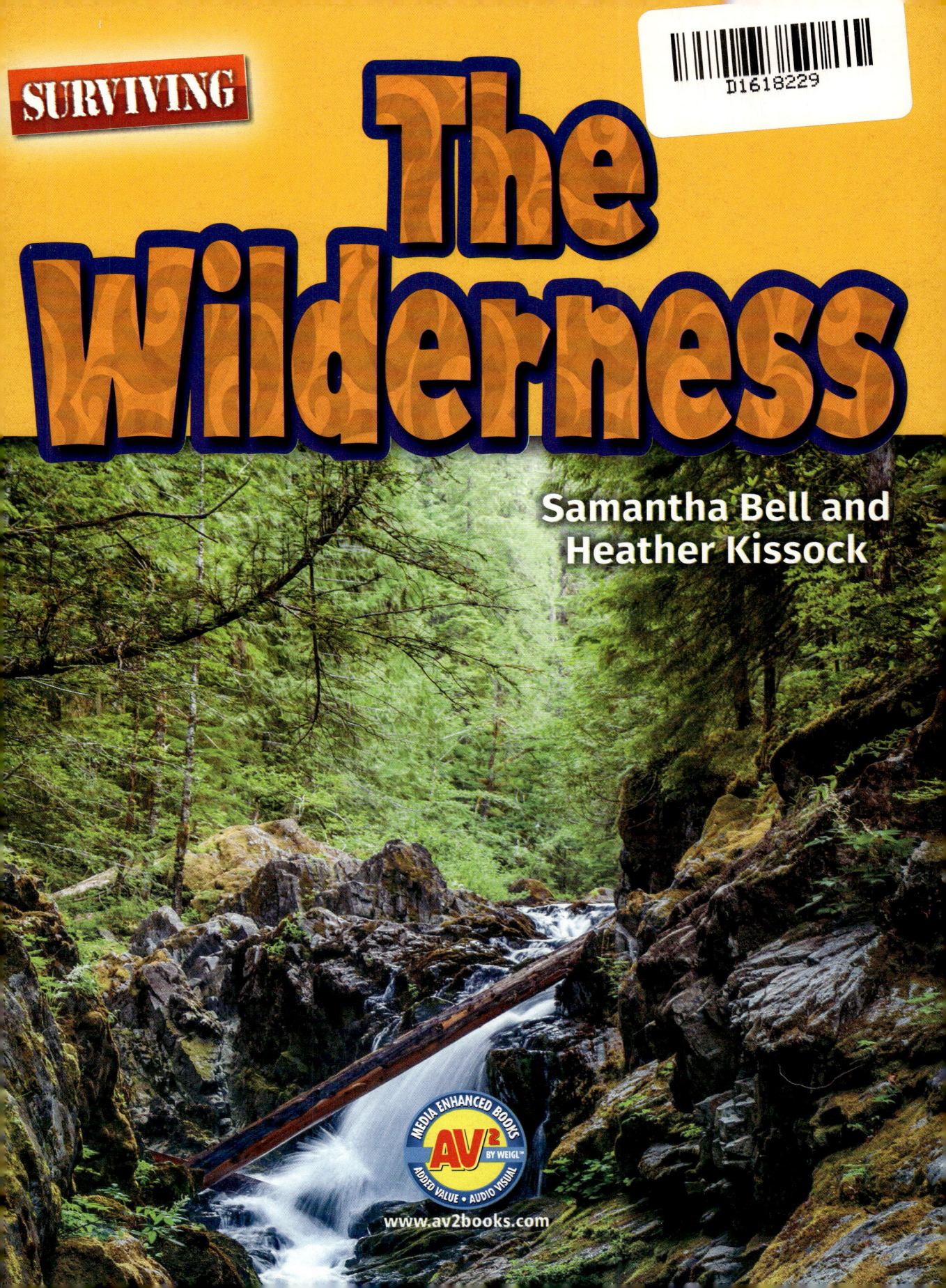
SURVIVING
The Wilderness

Samantha Bell and Heather Kissock

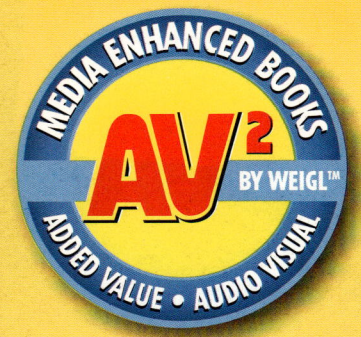

AV² provides enriched content that supplements and complements this book. Weigl's AV² books strive to create inspired learning and engage young minds in a total learning experience.

Your AV² Media Enhanced books come alive with...

 **Audio** Listen to sections of the book read aloud.

 **Key Words** Study vocabulary, and complete a matching word activity.

 **Video** Watch informative video clips.

 **Quizzes** Test your knowledge.

 **Embedded Weblinks** Gain additional information for research.

 **Slide Show** View images and captions, and prepare a presentation.

 **Try This!** Complete activities and hands-on experiments.

... and much, much more!

Go to www.av2books.com, and enter this book's unique code.

BOOK CODE

AVJ82756

AV² by Weigl brings you media enhanced books that support active learning.

Published by AV² by Weigl
350 5th Avenue, 59th Floor
New York, NY 10118
Website: www.av2books.com

Copyright © 2020 AV² by Weigl
All rights reserved. No part of this publication may be reproduced, stored in a retrieval system, or transmitted in any form or by any means, electronic, mechanical, photocopying, recording, or otherwise, without the prior written permission of the publisher.

Library of Congress Cataloging-in-Publication Data
Names: Bell, Samantha, author.
Title: The wilderness / Samantha Bell.
Description: New York, NY : AV2 by Weigl, 2019. | Series: Surviving |
  Includes index. | Audience: Grade 4 to 6.
Identifiers: LCCN 2018053483 (print) | LCCN 2018054737 (ebook) | ISBN
  9781489697998 (Multi User ebook) | ISBN 9781489698001 (Single User ebook)
  | ISBN 9781489697974 (hardcover : alk. paper) | ISBN 9781489697981
  (softcover : alk. paper)
Subjects: LCSH: Wilderness survival--Juvenile literature.
Classification: LCC GV200.5 (ebook) | LCC GV200.5 .B45 2019 (print) | DDC
  613.6/9--dc23
LC record available at https://lccn.loc.gov/2018053483

Printed in the United States of America in Brainerd, Minnesota
1 2 3 4 5 6 7 8 9 0   22 21 20 19 18

122018
120118

Project Coordinator: Heather Kissock   Designer: Ana María Vidal

Every reasonable effort has been made to trace ownership and to obtain permission to reprint copyright material. The publishers would be pleased to have any errors or omissions brought to their attention so that they may be corrected in subsequent printings.

Weigl acknowledges Alamy, Newscom, iStock, Shutterstock and Wikimedia as its primary image suppliers for this title.

First published by The Child's World in 2016.

The Wilderness

Contents

CHAPTER ONE
Waiting for Help 4

CHAPTER TWO
Keys to Survival 8

Timeline 15

CHAPTER THREE
Daily Tasks 16

Wilderness Rescue 21

Quiz 22

Key Words/Index 23

Log on to
www.av2books.com 24

Chapter 1

It rained when Penaflor was in the woods. He crawled under a big log to stay dry.

Waiting for Help

In September 2013, 72-year-old Gene Penaflor went hunting with a friend in a California forest. The two men went in different directions to track deer. They planned to meet for lunch. But Penaflor never came back.

Penaflor had walked about 2.5 miles (4 kilometers). He had not planned to go so far from the road. Suddenly, he slipped down a steep hill and hit his head hard. The impact knocked him unconscious.

When Penaflor awoke, he noticed he had a bad cut on his chin. But he had not broken any bones. He was not sure what time it was. A thick fog had rolled in. He did not know how to get back.

Penaflor knew he needed to stay in the area. He might never be found if he kept wandering. But he was high in the mountains. It was cold. He went downhill to set up camp but did not go any farther.

Penaflor had lost his knife but still had his rifle. He would need to get everything else from nature. He found a stream where he could get water. He was able to light a fire. Days passed. Sometimes, the temperature was below freezing. He put grass and leaves around his body for **insulation**.

Penaflor was too tired and weak to hunt large animals. But he shot squirrels and other small game with his gun. He ate lizards, frogs, and snakes that he caught. He scooped up algae from the water and ate that, too.

Protein

Your body needs protein to stay strong. Protein is the body's main building block for muscles, bones, hair, skin, and nails. It also helps the body fight against germs and organisms that can cause disease. In the wilderness, people can get protein by eating eggs, insects, fish, turtles, birds, and mammals.

Finally, after 19 days, a hunter wandered close to Penaflor's camp. Penaflor saw him and called for help. The hunter heard him and came to help. Penaflor was hungry, weak, and tired. But he was safe.

More than 100 people went out to look for Penaflor the day after he went missing.

It can be fun to experience nature through outdoor activities. Camping, hiking, skiing, rafting, and rock climbing offer lots of adventure. But nature is unpredictable. You should always be prepared for an emergency. That way, if disaster does strike, you will be ready to survive in the wilderness.

Insects contain **more protein** than chicken, beef, or fish.

Between **1992** and **2007**, there were **65,439** search and rescue incidents in U.S. National Parks.

A person **cannot live** for more than **7 days** without **water**.

Chapter 2

Many people bring electronic signals into the mountains. These can help rescuers find hikers if something goes wrong.

Keys to Survival

People have to survive in the wilderness for different reasons. Some people get lost. Like Penaflor, they might become confused and not be able to find their way back. Other times, people get caught in natural disasters like storms and avalanches. Sometimes, an accident will leave them stranded.

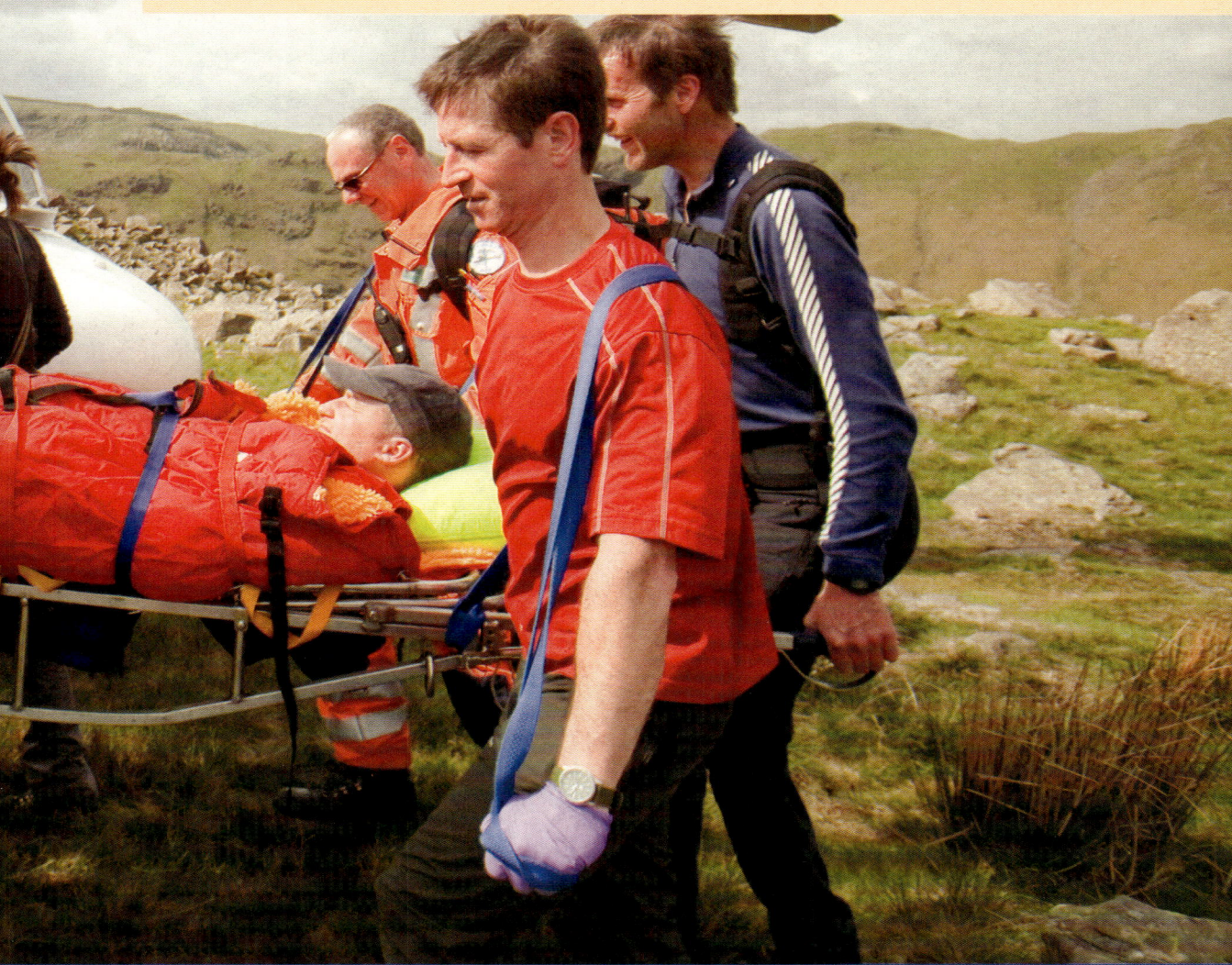

Supplies and outdoor skills can help a person survive in the wilderness. But the most important thing to have is a good attitude. People who are lost need to stay confident that they will get out.

In July 2003, Amy Racina was hiking by herself in the King's Canyon National Park in California. She walked off the trail near a **ravine**. The ground suddenly crumbled beneath her. Racina fell a long way down. She landed on some rocks. She broke both of her legs and one of her hips. But she did not give up. She pulled herself along with her hands for four days until some other hikers found her.

It is important to evaluate the situation when stuck in the wilderness. If you are lost, stay where you are. People are harder to find if they walk around. Move only if you need to find a safer location. If you must move, it is good to go to a place easy for rescuers to see.

Sometimes, people know the way out of the wilderness. But it takes them a while to get there. They might be hurt. Or it might be getting dark. In 1992, 25-year-old Colby Coombs was climbing Mount Foraker in Alaska. Before he reached the top, he was caught in an avalanche. He broke his ankle, shoulder blade, and two bones in his neck. It took him five days to get back down the mountain.

To survive in the wilderness, the first thing to do is build a shelter. A shelter helps protect from the sun, wind, rain, and snow. There are many different kinds of shelter.

Coombs had a tent with him. But a shelter can also be simple. An **evergreen** tree can protect you from wind or rain. In 2009, nine-year-old Grayson Wynne was separated from his family in Ashley National Forest. He remembered some survival tips he learned from a television show. Grayson created a small shelter under a fallen tree to keep himself dry.

People lost in the woods can use branches and sticks to create strong shelters.

Sometimes, survivors need extra warmth. Penaflor used leaves for insulation. But there are other ways to keep warm. In August 2014, 58-year-old Mike Vilhauer went fishing with friends. He wandered off to find grasshoppers to use as fishing bait. But he could not find his way back. The first two nights, he covered himself with pine needles and bark to stay warm. After that, he found a large rock to use as a shelter.

A sturdier shelter like a lean-to takes longer to set up. You can make one of these by forming a frame with larger branches and covering it with sticks or leaves. These kinds of shelters seem more like a home. They often help people keep a good attitude.

Some people surround fires with stones, clay, or mud. This helps keep the fire from getting out of control.

Snow is another good insulator. In a cold climate, you can dig a cave into a **snowdrift**. The cave should be big enough to lie down in. Grass, leaves, and brush on the floor of the cave can keep you off the snow.

In addition to a shelter, survivors often need a fire to stay warm. People use several different kinds of fuel to make fire. Tinder is thin, dry material that is easy to light. Bark, dry grass, and pine needles make good tinder. Kindling is a little bigger. Kindling consists of thin, dry branches about as thick as a pencil. Kindling helps the flame grow. Once there is a good flame, smaller branches can be added. Finally, larger branches are used to keep the fire burning. Dead branches from standing trees are best. Wood that has been sitting on the ground is often **damp** or wet.

Types of Wood for a Fire

There are many types of trees in the wilderness. Evergreens like cedar, spruce, and pine are softwood trees. Softwood trees usually contain sap. This makes the wood burn more quickly and give off more smoke than hardwood trees. Rescuers can easily spot smoky fires. Most trees with broad leaves, such as hickory, beech, and oak, have harder wood. It is often more difficult to light hardwoods. But they last longer. They also make hot coals that can be used later.

People lose water quickly when they are hiking. Finding a source of water is very important.

Once a survivor has a fire, the next thing to do is find water to drink. People can live only a few days without water. It is always good to **purify** water, even if only through a cloth. But you may need to drink water that is not completely clean. Staying **hydrated** is more important than avoiding unclean water.

Water moves downhill, so low areas will likely have a stream or small pool. People in colder areas can melt snow or ice. Others gather water when it rains.

In 2011, 40-year-old Bill Lawrence was hunting with friends when he got lost. His water ran out. But he was able to catch rainwater in his water bottle.

There is also water in the ground. You can look for places where the plants are bright green and dig there. Animals also need water. Tracks are another sign that water is close. After Lawrence drank his rainwater, he followed animal tracks and found a puddle.

Timeline

People can become lost in the wilderness under a range of circumstances and for a variety of reasons. Even with today's technology, people can still become lost in remote areas, with no way to contact those who could help.

1920 Three U.S. Navy personnel crash their balloon in Canada's Far North. With little food and equipment, they walk for a week before finding help.

1967 When his plane runs out of fuel, Bob Gauchie is forced to land on a remote lake in northern Canada. He spends 58 days in the brutal cold before being rescued.

1971 Juliane Koepcke, the only survivor of a plane crash in the Peruvian jungle, follows a small stream for nine days before arriving at a logger's camp, where she is rescued.

1981 After getting separated from his friends while exploring the Bolivian jungle, Yossi Ghinsberg wanders the Amazon Rainforest for 3 weeks, surviving on fruit and bird eggs. A search party finally finds him walking along a riverbank.

2003 While scrambling through a Utah canyon, Aron Ralston becomes wedged between a dislodged boulder and the canyon wall. After several days pass and no help arrives, Ralston amputates his own arm to free himself. Weak and near death, he is able to hike out of the canyon and find help.

2018 Angela Hernandez is driving along the California coast when she swerves to avoid an animal on the road. Her SUV goes over a cliff, landing 200 feet (61 meters) below the highway. Her vehicle filling with water, she breaks a window to get out. The next seven days are spent yelling for help from the cars passing above. Two hikers finally find her and call for help.

The Wilderness

Chapter 3

Deadly nightshade berries look similar to blueberries but are poisonous.

Daily Tasks

People can live for weeks without eating. But they will become weaker and weaker without food. It is always good to bring extra food into the wilderness. Trail mix is an easy, lightweight option that contains lots of energy. It is usually made up of nuts, seeds, dried fruit, and chocolate. Beef jerky and energy bars are other good foods to take hiking.

You may have to get your food from nature if you do not have any supplies to eat. It is important for people going into the wilderness to learn what they can eat in the area. That way, they do not eat something that will make them sick.

People in the wilderness often find fruit near their campsites. Lawrence ate **persimmons** he found on the ground. Berries are common, too. But some plants are poisonous. Avoid eating any unfamiliar plants.

Survivors can also search for animals to eat. Lawrence found some worms under a stump and ate them. Grasshoppers, crickets, and termites can be good to eat. Insects that have bright colors or give off a strong smell are not usually good to eat. Do not eat any animal unless you know that eating it will not harm you.

Hanging supplies between trees helps keep them away from bears and other animals.

Fish are a good food source. If you do not have a fishing hook and line, use what you have to make them. You can use the string from your clothes for line. You can bend a small piece of metal like a hook. Insects and worms make good bait. You can also create a spear from a branch or use clothing as a net.

Sometimes, people in the wilderness have supplies with them. It is important to keep supplies safe so they can be used.

Place food where animals cannot get it. Hang it high on a tree branch. If you cannot get the food into a tree, leave it at least 200 feet (61 m) from the campsite.

Survivors need to take care of themselves. They should try to wash every day. If there is not enough water, they can take an "air bath." This is when a person takes off as much clothing as possible and lays it out in the sun. The air helps the skin. The sun kills bacteria. It is also important to keep your feet dry. Feet can develop bad sores if wet for too long.

There are things you can do to make it easier for rescuers to find you. Use signals in open areas. Move around to attract attention. Wave your arms and run back and forth. Make a lot of noise. Use a whistle if you have one. A sound repeated three times means someone needs help.

Planes flying above can see light cloth, even if it is dark out. Wynne had a bright yellow raincoat. He tore it into strips to mark the path he took. He waved the last piece over his head when he saw the rescuers.

Avoiding Bad Bacteria

Bacteria are tiny organisms. You can only see them with a microscope. They live on food, plants, animals, and even people. Some bacteria are helpful. They help you **digest** food. But other bacteria can make you sick. Washing your hands is one of the best ways to get rid of bad bacteria. It is worth it to wash with water even if you do not have soap.

Some people create signal fires. Adding green branches and leaves will make smoke that can be seen for miles on a clear day. The fire will be easy to see on **overcast** days and at night. But be sure to keep your signal fire under control.

You can also use a mirror to signal for help. Glass and metal can flash the Sun's light for miles.

Signals on the ground can help, too. Use clothing or branches to make shapes on the ground. They will look out of place to people flying above.

The wilderness can seem like a dangerous place. But people of all ages have survived in it. They learned the importance of being prepared and never giving up.

Approximately **50 percent** of Americans are involved in **outdoor** activities.

Between 2008 and 2015, **1,610 people died** from animal encounters in the United States.

The U.S. National Parks Service **responds** to an average of **11 rescue calls per day**. Each rescue costs the service about **$900**.

Wilderness Rescue

Wilderness safety groups can be found around the world. They develop training programs, create technology, and organize search and rescue operations to help those stranded in remote areas.

United States Operating out of Centreville, Virginia, the National Association for Search and Rescue works to develop training programs for search and rescue workers nationwide.

South Africa Based in Cape Town, Wilderness Search and Rescue coordinates the search for, the medical treatment of, and rescue of people in wilderness environments.

Hong Kong Part of Hong Kong's Civil Aid Service, the Mountain Search and Rescue Company is responsible for the search and rescue of people missing in hiking and mountain activities.

Quiz

1 Where can people find protein in the wilderness?

2 For how long can a person live without water?

3 How much does it cost for the U.S. National Parks Service to respond to a call?

4 What is the first thing someone needs to do to survive in the wilderness?

5 What items can be used to create fuel for a fire?

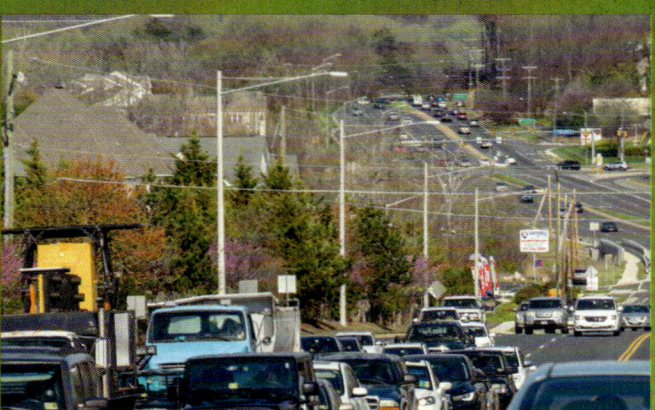

6 What are bacteria?

7 What are some good foods to take when hiking?

8 Where is the National Association for Search and Rescue based?

ANSWERS 1. Eggs, insects, fish, turtles, birds, and mammals **2.** No more than 7 days **3.** About $900 **4.** Build a shelter **5.** Bark, dry grass, pine needles, and branches **6.** Tiny organisms that live on food, plants, animals, and people **7.** Trail mix, beef jerky, and energy bars **8.** Centreville, Virginia

Key Words

damp: containing a small amount of liquid. Dew makes the ground feel damp.

digest: to change food into a simpler form so it can be used by the body. The body must digest food to get more energy.

evergreen: a tree that has leaves that stay green all year. A pine tree is an evergreen tree.

hydrated: when something has enough water. People must be hydrated to stay healthy.

insulation: material used to prevent something from losing heat. Leaves, bark, grass, and hay can be used as insulation.

overcast: very cloudy. An overcast sky hides the Sun.

persimmons: orange fruits that resemble plums. Persimmons are bitter before they are ripe.

purify: to make something clean. When you purify water, you get rid of bacteria.

ravine: a small, narrow valley with steep sides. You must be very careful if you hike near a ravine.

snowdrift: a bank or pile of windblown snow. You can dig deep into a snowdrift for shelter.

Index

accident 9
avalanche 9, 10

bacteria 19, 22
berries 16, 17

campsite 6, 17, 18
Coombs, Colby 10, 11

evergreen 11, 13

fire 6, 12, 13, 14, 20, 22
fishing 12, 18
food collection 17

hardwood 13
hygiene 19

insulation 6, 12, 13

kindling 13

Lawrence, Bill 14, 17
lean-to 12

Penaflor, Gene 4, 5, 6, 7, 9, 12
pine needles 12, 13, 22
positive attitude 10, 12
protein 6, 7, 22

Racina, Amy 10
rescue 7, 8, 10, 13, 15, 19, 20, 21, 22

shelter 11, 12, 22
signal 8, 19, 20
snowdrift 13
softwood 13
supplies 10, 17, 18

tent 11
tinder 13
trail mix 17, 22

Vilhauer, Mike 12

water collection 6, 14
water purification 14
Wynne, Grayson 11, 19

Log on to www.av2books.com

AV² by Weigl brings you media enhanced books that support active learning. Go to www.av2books.com, and enter the special code found on page 2 of this book. You will gain access to enriched and enhanced content that supplements and complements this book. Content includes video, audio, weblinks, quizzes, a slide show, and activities.

AV² Online Navigation

Audio
Listen to sections of the book read aloud.

Book Pages
AV² pages directly correspond to pages in the book.

Video
Watch informative video clips.

Key Words
Study vocabulary, and complete a matching word activity.

Embedded Weblinks
Gain additional information for research.

Try This!
Complete activities and hands-on experiments.

Quizzes
Test your knowledge.

Slide Show
View images and captions, and prepare a presentation.

AV² was built to bridge the gap between print and digital. We encourage you to tell us what you like and what you want to see in the future.

Sign up to be an AV² Ambassador at www.av2books.com/ambassador.

Due to the dynamic nature of the Internet, some of the URLs and activities provided as part of AV² by Weigl may have changed or ceased to exist. AV² by Weigl accepts no responsibility for any such changes. All media enhanced books are regularly monitored to update addresses and sites in a timely manner. Contact AV² by Weigl at 1-866-649-3445 or av2books@weigl.com with any questions, comments, or feedback.